I Know Who I Am

First published October 1991.

ISBN: 0-89486-781-4

Printed in the United States of America.

Library of Congress Catalog Card Number: 91-73227

ABOUT P. K. HALLINAN

Patrick Hallinan began writing children's books at the request of his wife, who asked him to create an original Christmas gift for their two young sons. Today, nearly twenty years later, P. K. Hallinan is one of America's foremost authors of children's books that teach personal values and self-esteem to young readers. His sensitive text and heart-warming illustrations offer a celebration of life to all who visit his very special world.

Although Mr. Hallinan writes primarily for children, his books manage to touch the child in all of us. It's this ability that enables Hallinan's books to be enjoyed by all children, young and old, who see the world through the eyes of innocence.

Mr. Hallinan lives with his wife, Jeanne, and their three dogs in Ashland, Oregon. He is the author of thirty children's books, including *Easy Does It, One Day at a Time, Live and Let Live, I Know There's a Power,* and *I Know I Belong*—all published by Hazelden Educational Materials.

I Know Who I Am

P.K. Hallinan

HAZELDEN®

I know who I am
and I'm happy to say
I like myself better
with each passing day.

Sometimes I'm silly.

Sometimes I'm sad.

There are times I get angry. . .

and times I feel glad.

I have lots of feelings;
they come and they go.
They all can be helpful,
they all help me grow.

I know who I am
because I'll always be
the one who is best
at just being me.

I like to be friendly
and to offer my hand.

I try to get help
when I don't understand.

And I've found that I'm able
to flourish and grow
by keeping life simple
and taking things slow.

I know who I am
and I've managed to see
my self-respect starts
when I'm honest with me.

We all have our limits,
we all have our flaws.

We all have to patch up
the problems we cause.

For tomorrow's adventures
are coming up fast,
and yesterday's shadows
should be left to the past.

I've stopped feeling greater
or lesser than those
whose lives may have led them
down different roads.

I've stopped holding grudges
and other harsh thoughts
that only undo
something good I've been taught.

I have my own interests,
I have my own views.

I like to choose friends
who have their own, too.

And this much is certain,
I always do fine
when I turn my life over
to patience and time.

Yes, I know who I am,
for I know that it's true:
Whatever my thoughts,
I can choose what I DO.

So I'll reach out to others
with what I can give.

And I'll try to be careful
to live and let live.

For each day will help me
to fill out my plan.

And my happiness tells me . . .

I know who I am.